The INSIDE GUIDE

STEM IN SPORTS

STEM in Baseball

By Beatrice Harris

Cavendish Square

Published in 2025 by Cavendish Square Publishing, LLC
2544 Clinton Street Buffalo, NY 14224

Website: cavendishsq.com

Library of Congress Cataloging-in-Publication Data

Names: Harris, Beatrice, author.
Title: STEM in baseball / Beatrice Harris.
Description: Buffalo, New York : Cavendish Square Publishing, [2025] |
Series: The inside guide: STEM in sports | Includes index.
Identifiers: LCCN 2023048674 (print) | LCCN 2023048675 (ebook) | ISBN 9781502671226 (library binding) | ISBN 9781502671219 (paperback) | ISBN 9781502671233 (ebook)
Subjects: LCSH: Baseball–Juvenile literature. | Science–Study and teaching–Juvenile literature. | Sports sciences–Juvenile literature.
Classification: LCC GV867.5 .H38 2025 (print) | LCC GV867.5 (ebook) | DDC 796.357–dc23/eng/20231101
LC record available at https://lccn.loc.gov/2023048674
LC ebook record available at https://lccn.loc.gov/2023048675

Editor: Therese Shea
Copyeditor: Danielle Haynes
Designer: Deanna Lepovich

The photographs in this book are used by permission and through the courtesy of: Cover zsolt_uveges/Shutterstock.com; p. 4 Eugene Onischenko/Shutterstock.com; p. 6 Jenny Solomon/Shutterstock.com; p. 7 wituli/Shutterstock.com; p. 8 VDB Photos/Shutterstock.com; p. 9 mTaira/Shutterstock.com; p. 10 James Steidl/Shutterstock.com; p. 12 Romaro Images/Shutterstock.com; p. 13 (main) Mike Orlov/Shutterstock.com; p. 13 (inset) HE Photography/Shutterstock.com; p. 15 Debby Wong/Shutterstock.com; p. 16 Will Hughes/Shutterstock.com; pp. 18 (top), 28 (bottom) Conor P. Fitzgerald/Shutterstock.com; p. 18 (bottom) Babe Ruth by Conlon, 1916/Wikimedia Commons; p. 19 Alison Young/Shutterstock.com; pp. 21, 29 (bottom) Andrey Yurlov/Shutterstock.com; pp. 22 (main), 27, 29 (top) PeopleImages.com - Yuri A/Shutterstock.com; p. 22 (inset) Prachaya Roekdeethaweesab/Shutterstock.com; p. 24 musa122/Shutterstock.com; pp. 25, 26 Suzanne Tucker/Shutterstock.com; p. 28 (top) Dennis Ku/Shutterstock.com.

CPSIA compliance information: Batch #CSCSQ25: For further information contact Cavendish Square Publishing LLC at 1-877-980-4450.

Printed in the United States of America

CONTENTS

Pro baseball players make use of their knowledge of science, technology, engineering, and math on the field, whether they're aware of it or not.

A STEM SPORT

Chapter One

Baseball is sometimes called the "national **pastime**" of the United States. Its history goes back to the 1800s, but it developed from even earlier ball games. It's a sport that millions of Americans—and other people around the world—love to play and watch.

Baseball fans might not think about it, but their favorite sport couldn't exist without STEM—science, technology, engineering, and math. STEM is at work everywhere on the field, and STEM knowledge helps us understand how the game works. For example, physics—the science that deals with matter and energy—aids us in comprehending how a batter can hit a home run. Do you want to know more? Let's learn more about baseball's STEM connections!

Fast Fact

The Society for American Baseball Research (SABR) uses statistics, history, and other kinds of research to study baseball.

Starting with Stats

If you're a baseball lover, you won't be surprised that baseball involves math. People have been keeping track of players' and teams' statistics since **professional** baseball began. A statistic, or stat, is a number that

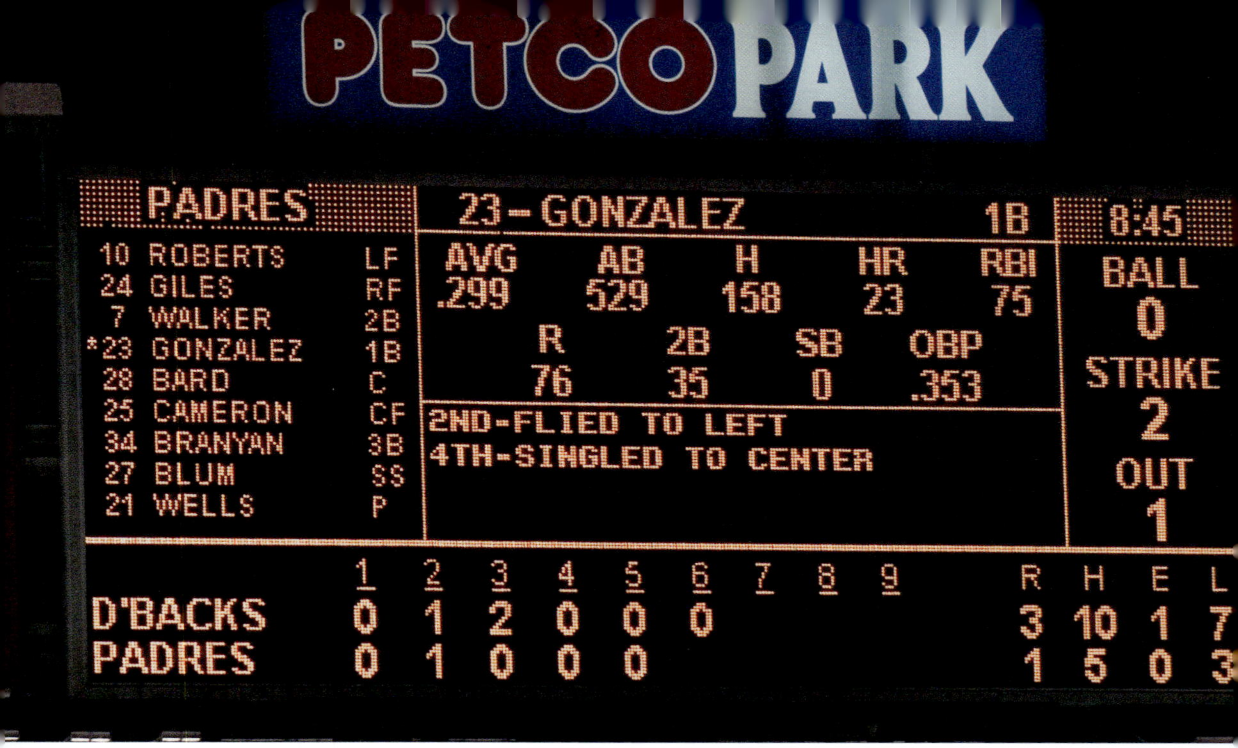

Fans can see stats on scoreboards like this.

stands for a piece of information. Stats are used in sports to compare players and teams, but they're especially important in baseball because the game is filled with so many numbers. People who study stats are called statisticians or analysts. To be a baseball statistician, you must be good at math.

Baseball statisticians figure out a lot of stats using **decimals**. For example, you can calculate a batting average by dividing the number of times a batter reaches a base through getting a hit by the number of total times they got a chance to hit (or their times "at-bat"). The result is a number between zero (.000) and

> **Fast Fact**
>
> Aroldis Chapman holds the Guinness World Record for fastest pitch as of 2023. He threw a fastball 105.8 miles (170 kilometers) per hour in 2010.

POWERFUL PITCHING

A pitcher's stats include how many runs they allow and how fast they throw a ball. Did you wonder how people measure ball speed? Engineers have developed technology to do this. One tool, called a radar gun, shoots a beam of **electromagnetic waves** called radio waves at the baseball. Once the waves hit the ball, they reflect back to the radar gun. The gun can use the changes in the reflecting waves to measure the ball's speed. A more recent radar system called TrackMan is used in many Major League Baseball (MLB) stadiums. TrackMan uses electromagnetic waves called microwaves.

Team scouts may use radar guns to check out a pitcher's fastball, which can be more than 100 miles (161 km) per hour.

Some fans keep track of the game themselves on scorecards.

one (1.000). Statisticians use computer programs to help them compare baseball stats too. However, it's still good to know how to use math on your own to compare the stats of your favorite baseball players.

Speed, Velocity, and Acceleration

In baseball, even the speed of a swing is measured and recorded. That measurement may be in miles or kilometers per hour.

You can also measure the bat's movement by its velocity. Speed and velocity are different. Speed measures distance over time, while velocity measures change in position over time. These are only the same quantities if an object travels in a straight path. Velocity also includes direction,

You can figure out speed, velocity, and acceleration using formulas. For example, speed is distance divided by time; velocity is the change in position divided by time; and acceleration is the change of velocity divided by time.

Fast Fact

A pro player can swing a bat as fast as 70 miles (113 km) per hour.

while speed doesn't. Sometimes sports announcers use speed and velocity to mean the same thing, though they shouldn't.

Another word announcers may use incorrectly is acceleration. They may use this to mean an increase in speed. However, accelerating actually means an object's velocity is changing over time (not just its speed). Acceleration can happen as a runner speeds up as they're rounding the bases on the way to home plate. However, acceleration can also mean slowing down! Like velocity, acceleration includes direction.

You'll always see the same shapes with the same measurements when you're at MLB ballparks. That makes the game fair for all the players no matter where they play.

Chapter Two

DIAMONDS AND SPHERES

Geometry is a kind of math that deals with shapes, sizes, angles, and **dimensions**. A baseball diamond can be viewed and understood with geometric ideas in mind.

Geometry at the Game

Picture a baseball field from above. Look at the bases in the infield. They form a shape that's often called a baseball diamond but could also be called a baseball rhombus. A rhombus is a shape with four equal sides and opposite angles that are equal to one another.

A baseball diamond could have another name too—a baseball square! A square is a kind of rhombus with four equal sides and four equal angles. All the lines between the bases on a baseball field are equal in length. All the angles between these lines are 90 degrees. Angles that measure 90 degrees are known as right angles. A square is a shape with four right angles.

Fast Fact

On a softball infield, there are 60 feet (18.3 meters) between bases. On a baseball infield, that distance is 90 feet (27.4 m).

What About the Ball?

You might be tempted to say that a baseball is a **sphere**. While it's round, it's not a perfect sphere because of its red stitching. This stitching affects how the ball is thrown, how it rolls, and how it acts when it's hit.

Check out this chart to see more measurements on an MLB field.

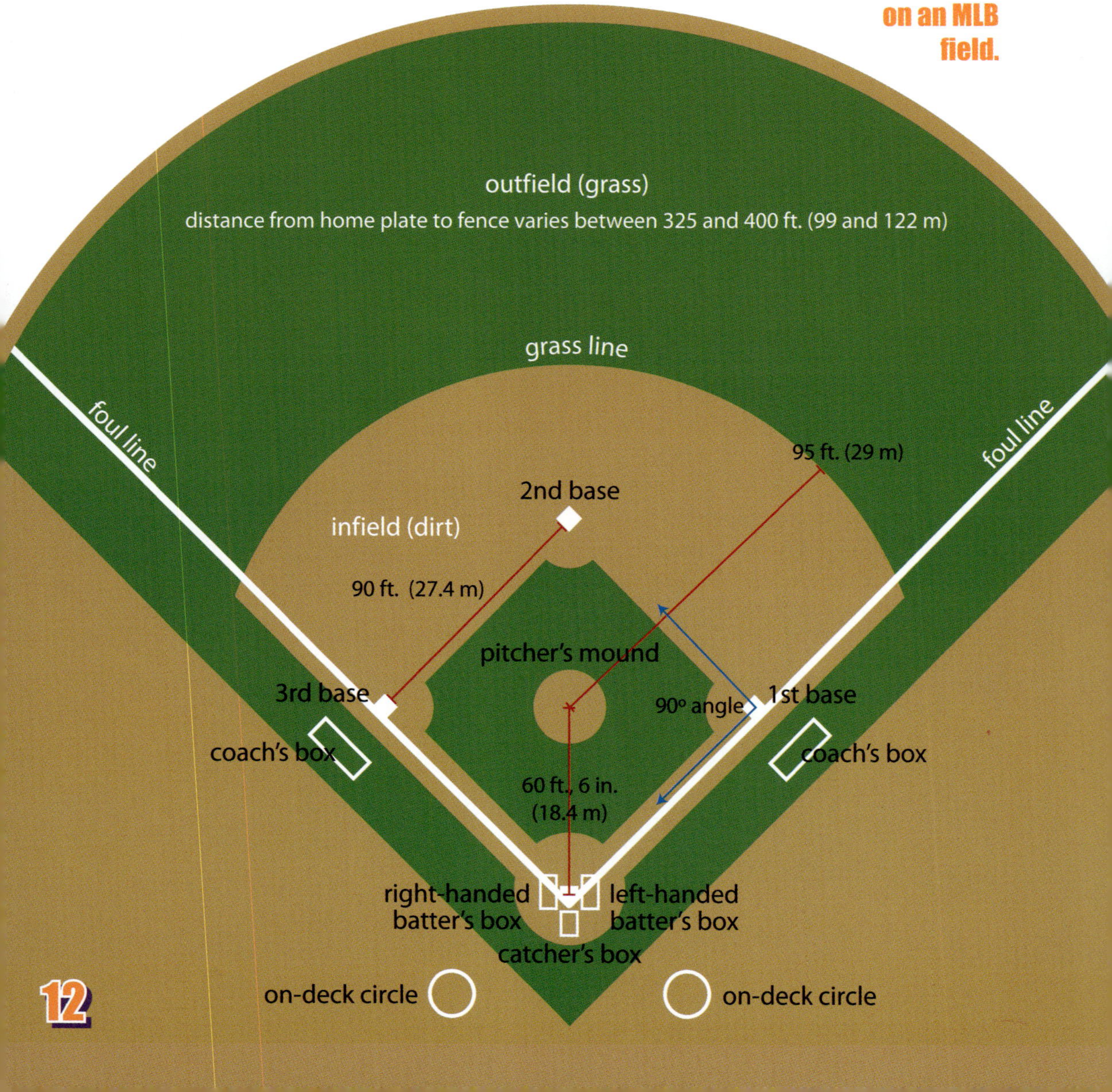

Pitchers can use air resistance, which is also called drag, to confuse hitters. Air resistance is a kind of friction.

Fast Fact

At the center of a baseball is a small ball of cork, a kind of light, bouncy wood, covered with rubber. Lots of yarn is wrapped around this core. The outside of the baseball is covered with leather and red stitching.

Pitchers can adjust the ball's movement using a force called air resistance. Air is made of molecules like everything else. When a ball moves through the air, the air molecules push back on it. Pitchers throw the ball differently to allow different parts of the stitching to catch the air. Air flows around

Baseballs for professional games usually have 108 double stitches, or 216 total stitches.

IT'S ILLEGAL

Some illegal pitches make a baseball even harder to hit. One of them is the spitball. A spitball is a baseball that has spit or another liquid on any part of the ball. The liquid changes the ball's aerodynamics and makes it move unevenly.

The slippery surface of a spitball makes the ball come out of the pitcher's hand more easily. This is because the liquid reduces friction between the pitcher's hand and the ball. Spitballs and other pitches that involve doctoring, or altering, the ball were banned from professional baseball in 1920.

Fast Fact

Weather matters at the park! A ball flying through humid air experiences less air resistance than one flying through dry air.

each area of the stitching, making the ball rise, curve, or drop. A branch of science called aerodynamics studies the way air moves around objects and the way objects move through the air.

Even though all baseballs are much the same, some factors can affect their performance in a game. One is wind. If the wind is going in the same direction as a baseball, it can push the ball farther. If the wind is pushing against the ball, the ball won't travel as far.

Air pressure also affects ball flight. Areas of high elevation have fewer air molecules than areas closer to sea level. This means they have lower air pressure. Coors Field in Denver, where the Colorado Rockies play, is at an elevation of 5,280 feet (1,609 m). It's easier to hit a home run there than it is in almost every other baseball stadium. There are fewer air molecules pushing on the ball and resisting its motion.

Baseball players might experience shortness of breath at higher elevations. Lower air pressure means less oxygen in the air.

Baseball equipment is designed to make good performances even better.

GEAR OF THE GAME

Chapter Three

You could play baseball with any equipment, but the best gear can be the difference between a single and a home run or between a catch and an error. The right gear can also keep players safe from injury. Let's see how STEM applies to baseball equipment.

Batter Up

The heavier the baseball bat, the more mass it has. Mass is how much matter is in an object. Mass might sound like weight, but weight depends on the force of gravity. A baseball bat that weighs 2 pounds (0.9 kilogram) on Earth will weigh a different amount on a planet with weaker or stronger gravity. The bat's mass, however, will remain the same.

The more mass an object has, the more force is needed to put it in motion. Applied force is a force that one object applies to another. A baseball player swings their arms to apply force to the bat. The player needs to use more force to swing a bat with more mass.

Fast Fact

Heavier bats deliver a more powerful swing. However, they're harder to swing because more force is needed to move them.

A baseball bat is smooth. Players sometimes put pine tar on it to grip it better. The pine tar creates friction between a player's hands and the smooth wood.

Glove or Mitt?

Most baseball gloves have the same basic design—except for those worn by the first baseman and catcher. The first baseman's glove,

Baseball legend Babe Ruth used a long, heavy bat—36 inches (91 centimeters) and over 3 pounds (1.3 kg). Most players today use shorter, lighter bats.